Cities through Time

Daily Life in
Ancient and Modern

by Joan Barghusen

illustrations by Ray Webb

℞

Runestone Press/Minneapolis
A Division of the Lerner Publishing Group

Copyright © 1999 by Runestone Press

The *Cities through Time* series is produced by Runestone Press, a division of the Lerner Publishing Group, in cooperation with Greenleaf Publishing, Inc., Geneva, Illinois.

Cover design by Michael Tacheny
Text design by Melanie Lawson

The Lerner Publishing Group
241 First Avenue North
Minneapolis, Minnesota 55401

Website address: www.lernerbooks.com

Library of Congress Cataloging-in-Publication Data

Barghusen, Joan D., 1935–
    Daily life in ancient and modern Rome / by Joan Barghusen ;
illustrations by Ray Webb.
        p. cm. — (Cities through time)
    Includes index.
    Summary: A historical exploration of events and daily life in Rome in
both ancient and modern times.
    ISBN 0–8225–3213–1 (lib. bdg. : alk. paper)
    1. Rome (Italy)—History—Juvenile literature. 2. Rome—History
—Juvenile literature. 3. Rome—Social life and customs—Juvenile
literature. 4. Rome (Italy)—Social life and customs—Juvenile
literature. [1. Rome. 2. Rome (Italy)] I. Webb, Ray, ill.
    II. Title. III. Series.
DG78.B34 1999
945—dc21   98–18311

Manufactured in the United States of America
1 2 3 4 5 6 – JR – 04 03 02 01 00 99

Contents

Introduction

Rome, called the "city of the seven hills," began as a tiny settlement of mud-walled dwellings overlooking the Tiber River. According to tradition, the legendary hero Romulus founded the city in 753 B.C. By the sixth century B.C., the Etruscans, a people from northern Italy, were dominating the young city and were transforming it into a prosperous urban area. By 509 B.C., the people of Rome had thrown off Etruscan rule and had established their own government, the Roman Republic.

Within five centuries, Roman armies had conquered lands not only around the Mediterranean Sea but also in western Europe and in Britain. In 27 B.C., Rome gave up its republican form of government and accepted the rule of an emperor. As the hub of the empire, the city spread Roman culture and, later, the Roman Catholic religion throughout the region. At its height, Rome held about a million people. Even after Rome's last emperor was deposed by northern invaders in A.D. 476, the city continued to be important as the center of the Roman Catholic Church. The pope, also known as the bishop of Rome, became the leader of western Christianity, and St. Peter's Basilica on Vatican Hill emerged as one of Christianity's most sacred shrines.

For centuries Rome has attracted pilgrims and tourists. The ancient ruins and glorious past of the "Eternal City" have long inspired artists, architects, and writers. Modern Rome is the capital of the Republic of Italy. Within the city limits lies Vatican City, an independent country created in 1929 with the pope as its ruler.

Over time, as Rome grew, evidence of its earliest inhabitants disappeared. But archaeologists have uncovered foundations of the dwellings where farmers and shepherds lived in the eighth century B.C. And they have found the remains of a cemetery where these early Romans buried their dead. Located in a valley between two hills, this cemetery lies below the Forum, the heart of ancient Rome.

Home and Public Life

The Forum, or marketplace, was the center of public life. From stalls that lined the square, food vendors and artisans offered their wares. Senators passed through the open square on their way to the Senate House, where they met to govern the city and the ever-increasing lands it controlled. In the Forum stood the Rostra, where speakers addressed the citizens to ask their support for election to high offices or to rally them to important state causes.

Senators came from the patrician class, which was made up of wealthy landowners who did not work for wages. Ordinary folk, or plebeians, worked as craftspeople, traders, or at some other wage-earning job. While any free-born Roman was a citizen, not all citizens had the same rights. A plebeian, for example, could not sit in the Senate. Plebeians had an assembly house of their own, but any decisions they made were only recommendations, not laws. Real political power rested with the senators.

Women could not vote and were barred from public life. In the ancient Roman view, a woman's proper role was in the home, where she and her children were subject to the authority of the *paterfamilias* (the male head of the household). Yet the Roman matron, who was wife and mother of the traditional family, was an important and respected member of society. She managed the household slaves or servants, supervised the spinning of wool for weaving, educated the family's young children, and trained her daughters as future matrons.

The paterfamilias acted as judge in family disputes and in conflicts with other families. He had the power of life and death over his wife and children. When a child was born, the infant was laid before the father to accept or reject, as he chose. A rejected infant was killed or abandoned. Ancestors were remembered and revered.

A young lawyer named Terentius Neo and his wife posed for a serious portrait early in their marriage.

Roman Religion

The ancient Romans saw gods everywhere. They revered spirits, or *numina,* residing in objects, places, or natural forces. And they worshiped a pantheon of gods and goddesses headed by Jupiter and his wife Juno. They honored their deities with offerings, usually of food, wine, or oil. For some rituals, animals were slaughtered as blood sacrifices.

The Romans believed that a ritual must be performed exactly before they could hope for the expected outcome. Before any important event—such as a wedding, a journey, or a battle—the Romans tried to find out if the gods approved. To learn the will of the gods, they consulted oracles, fortune-tellers, or the Sibylline books (the sacred writings of a prophetess). They might also ask the advice of an augur priest, who read omens in the flights of birds, or of a *haruspex,* who divined omens in the entrails of slaughtered animals.

Every household had its own protective gods, called *lares.* The paterfamilias, acting as priest, made offerings of food, wine, oil, or cakes on the altar of the household shrine or threw food into the hearth fire to be consumed by the gods.

Just as each home had a hearth, the state had a sacred hearth. In a small building near the Forum, priestesses of the goddess Vesta tended an eternal flame, which could not be allowed to go out for fear that harm would come to Rome. A priestess who let the eternal flame die could be put to death. The temple of Jupiter in central Rome was important for state and business functions. For example, to make an agreement binding, both parties swore an oath of good faith before Jupiter. And victorious generals marched in triumph to Jupiter's altar.

This procession of the vestal virgins was depicted by a nineteenth-century painter. The vestal virgins had the task of keeping the eternal flame alive. They served for as long as 30 years.

"My prayers will be fulfilled. Do you see how the prophetic liver among the favorable entrails announces that the gods are propitious?"
—Tibellus, on purifying the crops and fields

Afternoon at the Circus

More than 250,000 Romans could be seated at the Circus Maximus, the oldest and largest arena for public games. Chariot racing was the most popular sport. Chariots circled seven times around the long, oval track, turning dangerously around the wooden posts that marked each end of the course. The noise was deafening as spectators cheered their favorite chariot drivers. Adding to the excitement was the possibility that money could be won or lost, for betting was allowed.

Four factions, or stables, provided the horses and drivers. Their staffs included trainers, grooms, stableboys, veterinarians, saddlers, and guards. But the glory went to the charioteers. Recognizable from the far reaches of the crowd by the color of his tunic, the charioteer was a skilled athlete, admired for his ability and daring. Usually low-born, perhaps even a slave, the chariot driver spent years in training. Victory was often rewarded with honor, prestige, and a following of fans, who sometimes scrawled the driver's name in public places. If successful, the charioteer could make a fortune—or win freedom from slavery—through victory gifts.

Wealthy state officials organized the games on a special holiday when business was forbidden. By one count, there were 93 of these days in a single year. The games began at a signal from the presiding official, who dropped a white handkerchief into the arena. Many races or other sports filled the day's program. According to Roman writers, an afternoon at the circus was also an occasion for flirting and romance. Many pleasures besides the games were offered. Foodsellers and fortune-tellers tempted buyers. All manner of vendors set up their wares in the arcades and market stalls outside the arena.

At the circus, men and women mingled freely. Chariot racing was an exciting feature of the Circus Maximus *(inset)*.

Streets of Rome

Rome was covered with a network of narrow, steep, and winding public pathways. Many had been used since the rural beginnings of the city and were little more than paths for foot travelers. Some were wide enough for a cart, but only a few broadened to the necessary 15 feet to allow two carts to pass.

As Rome grew, its streets became pinched and crowded. Single-family homes were only for the wealthy. More and more Romans lived in small apartments in large block buildings as high as five or six stories. Often poorly built, these buildings of timber and mud brick sometimes collapsed, endangering residents and passersby.

At the ground level, buildings were occupied by shops that opened onto the street. Here artisans, craftspeople, and shopkeepers manufactured and sold their products. Residents tossed into the streets the garbage and waste water from these shops, along with the refuse from apartments above.

Customers thronged to the bakeries, the meat markets, the barbers, the booksellers, and all the various merchants and vendors that a big city offers. The activity of shops often spilled outdoors, crowding the already narrow public ways. Apartment dwellers escaping their cramped quarters added to the crowds. And children played where they could, dodging the sedan chairs that carried the wealthy and the carts that hauled supplies through the city. As Rome grew, its streets became noisier, smellier, and more cramped. Carts and draft animals posed a danger to pedestrians. And with no effective garbage collection, refuse was left to rot in the street.

Although some main streets were paved with bricks, many smaller streets and alleys were not. In the summer, they turned to dust, and in the rain, to mud. Difficult by day, travel was even more hazardous at night. Lacking street lamps, the people of Rome had to carry torches or oil lamps to guide their way.

Romans could buy foodstuffs from a sidestreet stall *(inset)* or enjoy the lively entertainment near the Forum *(left)*.

13

The Roman Army

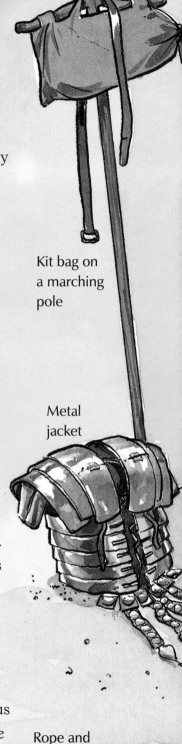

Kit bag on a marching pole

Metal jacket

Rope and chain

In the early years of the city, Roman soldiers had been citizens and property owners. They furnished their own armor, weapons, and food. After each campaign, they returned home again.

But over the centuries, as Rome dominated the surrounding towns of Italy, the citizen army grew into a full-time professional force. Men between the ages of 17 and 46 were eligible to serve, whether or not they owned property. By 146 B.C., when the Romans destroyed Carthage (in North Africa) to control the western Mediterranean, many soldiers were not Roman citizens. Instead the soldiers were recruited from the lands the armies entered. The Roman Republic equipped the recruits with weapons and supplies and paid them for their services. They could march 18 miles a day carrying the basic kit of equipment *(right)* weighing 60 pounds. A soldier could volunteer year after year for a maximum of 16 years. Many young men found that a military career helped them advance in society. Veterans were often rewarded with gifts of money or land or even the privilege of Roman citizenship. For men aspiring to high office, military service was a necessity.

When the armies of the Roman general Julius Caesar conquered Gaul (modern France), Rome added a big chunk of western Europe to its vast territories. But senators feared Caesar's ambition to become dictator and assassinated him in 44 B.C. For a decade, competing generals, supported by their armies, fought for the leadership of Rome. Octavian, later called Augustus, was the victor, and one of his first acts was to reorganize the army.

Under the reforms of Augustus, laws required soldiers to serve for 20 years of active duty and for 4 years in the reserves. The Roman government gave the soldiers pensions when they were discharged. Although they could not marry legally while in service, many took common-law wives, and often their sons became soldiers, too. Augustus formed the Praetorian Guard to serve as his bodyguard. This elite force had many privileges, including higher pay than ordinary soldiers and special uniforms. They were the only soldiers stationed in Rome.

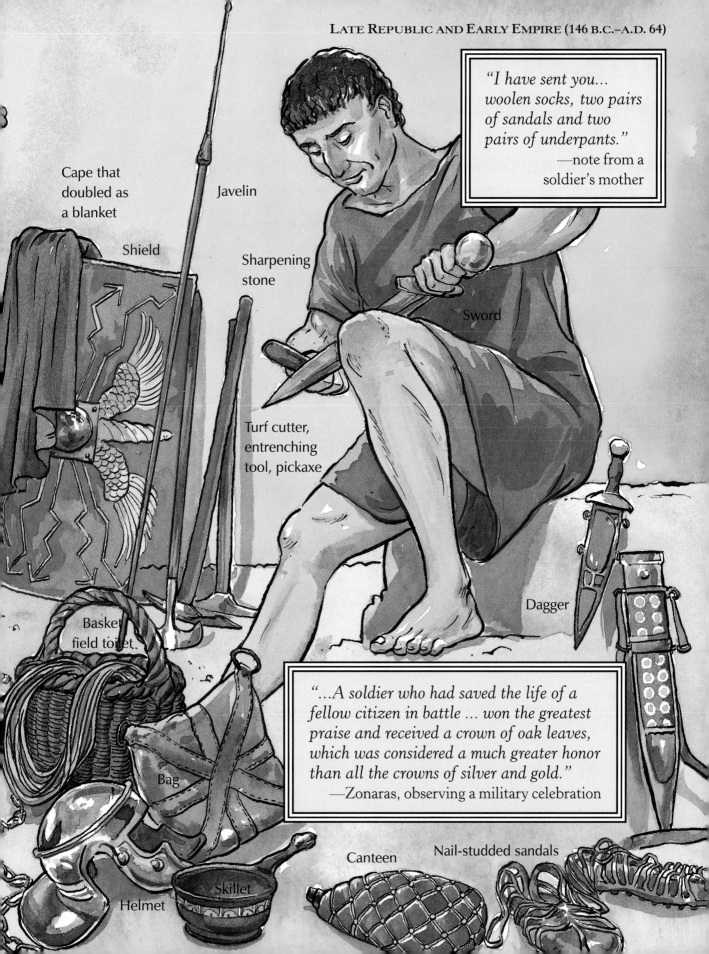

Cape that doubled as a blanket

Javelin

Shield

Sharpening stone

Sword

"I have sent you... woolen socks, two pairs of sandals and two pairs of underpants."
—note from a soldier's mother

Turf cutter, entrenching tool, pickaxe

Dagger

Basket field toilet

Bag

"...A soldier who had saved the life of a fellow citizen in battle ... won the greatest praise and received a crown of oak leaves, which was considered a much greater honor than all the crowns of silver and gold."
—Zonaras, observing a military celebration

Canteen

Nail-studded sandals

Skillet

Helmet

Slaves in Rome

Rome had always had a small slave population, which was made up of prisoners of war or citizens who had been sold to pay debts. As the victorious Roman armies captured more prisoners, however, the city's slave auctions expanded to include captives from many lands, including Greece. As a result, the number of slaves increased dramatically.

Keeping slaves under control was a major concern for Roman officials. In fact slave revolts inspired fear throughout the Roman world. Laws severely punished any acts of violence or rebellion against the slaveowner. If an owner was murdered by a slave, the law required that all the owner's slaves be put to death. Few rules curbed the master's authority. Slaves belonged to their owners, and they were treated kindly or harshly, depending on the master. Owners could put slaves to death at will. Some owners sold their slaves to gladiator schools, where the slaves would be trained for dangerous fights in the arena. In the early empire, the state limited these practices, but centuries passed before they became illegal.

Slaves often worked at hard manual labor in mining, manufacturing, agriculture, or construction. Some slaves belonged to the city. But many were household slaves, often with lighter tasks. If skilled, they might be barbers, hairdressers, cooks, or weavers. An educated slave might oversee other slaves in the household, might manage the owner's business or country estate, or might tutor the owner's children. Many tutors and doctors were Greek slaves.

Slaves could not legally marry, and any relationships they had could be broken up through sale and separation. Yet, many did have families, and the children belonged to the owner.

Slaves could be freed by purchase or by the master voluntarily letting go of the slave. Some masters, upon their death, released their slaves. Freed men and freed women received only limited rights of citizenship, but their descendants became full Roman citizens.

A master frees his slave.

Accountant

Masseur

Housemaid

Nursemaid

"*I have run away. Capture me. When you have returned me to my master, Zoninus, you will receive a reward.*"
—Inscription on a slave collar

Departing ships were loaded with smashed pots as ballast.

Pots called amphorae carried grain, wine, and olive oil.

Officials checked cargo and charged tribute for imports.

Treadmill crane

"You, Roman, do not fail to govern all people with your supreme authority. These will be your skills: to establish law and order within a framework of peace...."
—Virgil, *The Aeneid*

The Age of Augustus

The reign of Augustus (27 B.C. to A.D. 14) marked the beginning of the Roman Empire. Peace and prosperity came to Rome, and riches flowed in from vast conquered lands.

Boats crowded the docks along the Tiber, bringing products inland from Ostia, Rome's port on the Mediterranean Sea. Dockworkers unloaded huge clay jars filled with wine, oil, and grain. Gold and silver luxury items and manufactured goods were imported from North Africa, Spain, and the cities of the Mediterranean. New provinces provided sources for timber and stone so that beautiful marble could be imported for state building projects. Augustus restored and constructed so many buildings that he claimed to have found Rome a "city of brick" and to have left it a "city of marble."

The Romans had long admired the art and literature of Greece, a culture older than their own. Wealthy Romans brought in Greek artists to design and decorate buildings. And even though Latin was the language of the empire, tutors conducted lessons beyond simple reading, writing, and arithmetic in Greek. Educated Romans admired the ancient Greek authors, especially Homer, author of *The Iliad* and *The Odyssey,* long poems that glorified ancient Greek heroes.

During the reign of Augustus, the Roman poet Virgil composed an epic to celebrate the heroic beginnings of Rome. Although Virgil wrote in Latin, he adopted the Homeric style for his poem *The Aeneid.* It relates the story of Aeneas, whose destiny brought him to Italy.

Augustus wanted to reform society to be like "the good old days" of the Roman Republic. Concerned that the birthrate had dropped, especially among the upper classes, he passed laws to encourage more marriages. He provided rewards for parents who had three or more children and set financial penalties for those who did not marry. In spite of his efforts, no evidence exists that the birthrate among the upper classes increased, although increases had occurred among other social groups.

New wealth meant building with marble, not brick.

Dinner for Rich and Poor

Dinner for the wealthiest Romans was lavish. Elegantly prepared by fine cooks and pastry makers, the meal was served on tables surrounded by couches, where the family and guests reclined in comfort. The main course featured meat, perhaps pork, goose, chicken, fish, hare, wild game or birds. Roasted, boiled, or grilled, meats were often served in fruit or vinegar sauces or flavored with the popular fish paste called *garum*. Vegetables of many kinds, usually grown in home gardens, were plentiful. For dessert, there were figs, plums, apples, and grapes, as well as nuts and honey.

For the wealthy, breads and cakes were baked in novel shapes. Wine could be cooled in snow brought down from the mountains. Knives and spoons were

While the rich enjoyed lavish banquets *(right),* the poor, who often had no place to cook, resorted to cheap cookshops *(below).*

beautifully made of bronze, gold, and silver. Plates and cups might also be of metal or sometimes of glass. Slaves stood nearby with water for greasy fingers.

The servants and slaves in a wealthy household probably ate well, sharing in the master's leftovers. But for the poor of Rome, the staple of their diet was wheat, either baked into bread or cooked into a gruel. In cramped, kitchenless rooms, poor citizens could do little cooking beyond boiling wheat in a pot on a charcoal brazier. Olive oil, a little cheese, ordinary vegetables, and cheap wine probably completed their meal on most occasions. Those with a little money could purchase food already cooked from street vendors.

Monthly wheat rations from the Annona, Rome's yearly grain supply, helped Rome's poorest people, who depended on this charity to survive. And the state relied on the Annona to keep hungry crowds from rioting. Lists show that sometimes as many as 200,000—one of five Roman citizens—were eligible for wheat rations.

Foreign Religions

The Romans were tolerant of the gods of other peoples and sometimes even welcomed them. Before a battle, Roman generals invited the gods of the cities they attacked to come over to the Roman cause. At times of crisis, state officials had even looked to foreign deities for help.

Worship of Aesculapius, the Greek god of medicine, had begun during a plague in the third century B.C. A temple was built for him on Tiber Island, where the sick came seeking cures and doctors came to learn their trade. A statue of the Phrygian goddess Cybele had been brought to Rome in 204 B.C., when prophecies foretold that her presence could protect Rome in the dark days of war with Carthage. A crowd of Roman matrons who traveled to the coast of Italy welcomed the ship.

Many foreign gods came to Rome with the slaves who worshiped them and then attracted Roman citizens as well. The religions of the eastern Mediterranean, which promised to share the secrets of immortality or rebirth, were especially popular. Worship of the great Egyptian goddess Isis, often shown holding her infant son Horus, was widespread.

To show loyalty to Rome, the worshipers of non-Roman deities often made sacrifices to Jupiter or to the cult of the Roman emperor. But Judaism, brought to the city from the eastern Mediterranean, was a one-god faith. And so was the new religion of Christianity. Because Christians and Jews did not sacrifice to traditional Roman gods, Roman officials often viewed them with suspicion.

Christianity was based on the teachings of Jesus of Nazareth, who was born in Roman-controlled Palestine during the reign of Augustus. The new religion spread quickly throughout the empire, and Rome itself was home to a very early community of Christians. According to tradition, both Peter and Paul, two of Jesus' apostles, came to Rome during the middle of the first century A.D.

Egyptian gods were
among the many
foreign deities Romans
freely appealed to.

"The whole city had turned
out to meet her [Cybele],
and incense burners had
been placed in front of the
doorways along the route...."
—Livy

23

"The movement of heavy wagons through narrow streets, the oaths of stalled cattle drovers would break the sleep of a deaf man or a lazy walrus."
—Juvenal

Stepping stones for crossing muddy street

Public fountain

These tenements seldom had heating or running water above the first floors, so most citizens had neither indoor kitchens nor bathrooms. Many people used charcoal braziers for cooking or to keep warm in the winter. These open flames, as well as oil lamps, caused many fires. To provide more protection for the city, Augustus organized a brigade of 3,500 to 7,000 firefighters.

The City Grows

Historians estimate that one million people were living in Rome by the early years of the empire. The area enclosed within Rome's ancient walls no longer provided enough space for the growing city. Rome's population had begun to increase, and so had the amount of land taken up by public buildings. Settlements had spilled over the walls in all directions. The areas where poor citizens and freed people could afford to live became ever more cramped. With no place to build except up, apartment buildings grew dangerously high. Because of the danger of collapse, Augustus set a limit of 60 feet for the height of new structures.

Much of Rome's life took place on its streets. Even schoolteachers, paid by the parents of their students, often held classes on the street. In the shade of some building, amid noise and traffic, boys and girls would be expected to learn their lessons. To relieve congestion, laws banned wheeled traffic of most kinds from the streets in the daytime. However, the laws merely added to the noise that kept Romans awake, as carts bumped through the city by night.

To enjoy more open space, citizens could visit the Campus Martius, the low-lying region along the river outside the city walls. Here, sheltered from sun or rain, they could stroll under the roofed porticoes of temples or markets. Children could play around the giant obelisk that served as a sundial, casting its shadow on a pavement marked with the hours.

Outdoor school

Rome in Flames

The Great Fire of Rome *(right)* raged for six days and nights in the summer of A.D. 64, during the reign of the emperor Nero. No one knew how the fire started. The first flames spilled from wooden marketstalls outside the Circus Maximus. Fanned by wind, the fire spread quickly, and firefighters were powerless to stop it. At last it burned itself out, only to spring up again in other parts of the city.

The fire destroyed 10 of Rome's 14 regions. The loss of life and property stunned the people of the city. Refugees were sheltered in the Campus Martius and in Nero's own gardens on Vatican Hill. Rations were brought from Ostia, and the price of grain was lowered as a relief measure.

Nero was an unpopular ruler. In spite of the fact that he had been out of town when the fire started, people began to say that the emperor had set it. To turn away blame, Nero accused the Christians of the deed. They were a small group, already under political suspicion, and defenseless before the emperor's charges. Many Christians were executed in public spectacles held in Nero's gardens, with the emperor in attendance. Some Christians were torn apart by starved animals, and some were burned as human torches. So dreadful were their deaths, say historians, that many Romans were moved to pity the victims.

On land cleared by the fire, Nero began to build his Golden House, a grand residence in the center of the city. Its private gardens and lake covered so much land that one writer commented, "Nero has robbed the poor of places to live."

"Terrified, shrieking women, helpless old and young, people intent on their own safety, people unselfishly supporting invalids or waiting for them, fugitives and lingerers alike—all heightened the confusion. When people looked back, menacing flames sprang up before them or outflanked them. When they escaped to a neighboring quarter, the fire followed: even districts believed remote proved to be involved. Finally, with no idea where or what to flee, they crowded onto the country roads, or lay in the fields." —Tacitus

"All niceties were put aside, and it was pure and simple murder. The combatants have absolutely no protection....Each never fails to injure his opponent."
—Seneca the Younger, on combats between condemned prisoners

Spectacles in the Colosseum

For centuries Romans had watched sports, games, and all kinds of public spectacles in the Circus Maximus, the Forum, or any suitably large, open space. The huge Flavian Amphitheater, later nicknamed the "Colosseum," was constructed especially for state-sponsored exhibitions of armed combat, wild animal games, and public executions.

The new amphitheater could hold almost 50,000 spectators. Tokens were distributed to admit citizens free of charge, but social status determined seating. Women could sit only in the third, or uppermost, tier of seats. Slaves stood at the back.

As the crowd assembled, gladiators waited in cells under the arena floor for their turn to perform in bloody struggles that often ended in death. Gladiators were usually war captives, slaves, or criminals. Under the watchful eye of guards, they lived and trained in special gladiator schools run for the profit of their owners. In the gladiator games, men sometimes boxed or wrestled. More often they were equipped with sword, spear, slingshot, or dagger. Some gladiators fought with nets, which they used to entangle their opponents.

Urged on by noisy crowds, the combatants tested their skills and strength. Many died in the dangerous games, but those who were victorious became popular heroes. Fans kept track of the wins and losses of their favorites, and victors might finally be granted their freedom. Spectacles often included public executions, where prisoners were bound to stakes and torn apart by starving animals.

Lions, panthers, bears, and even elephants were imported to die in the spectacles *(left)*. At the Flavian Amphitheater's opening festivals, which lasted for 100 days in A.D. 80, nearly 10,000 animals were killed. Some arenas could even be flooded for mock naval battles *(inset)*.

Public Baths

O nly wealthy Romans had baths in their homes. Other citizens used the public baths scattered throughout the city. Many of these structures were small and dark, crammed into the blocks of tall apartment buildings.

But public baths built by the emperors were large and luxurious. New aqueducts supplied plenty of water, and improved methods of heating warmed the pools and rooms. With exercise rooms, meeting rooms, and sometimes even libraries added, baths became centers of social activity.

By the third century A.D., a citizen could visit the Baths of Caracalla, which had opened in A.D. 217. These enormous baths could accommodate 1,600 people, and almost everyone could afford to come. The very small fee was sometimes waived altogether, and children entered free. Set among formal gardens, the baths were splendidly decorated with marble walls, mosaic floors, and fine sculptures.

Although separate dressing rooms and exercise spaces existed for men and women, there was only one set of bathing pools. For this reason, women usually bathed in the morning and men in the afternoon, after their day's work was done.

Many bathers exercised first, playing ball, jogging, or wrestling. Those who could afford it might have a massage. For bathing, there were hot, warm, and cold pools, with small cubicles for people who wished to bathe in private. For swimmers, there was an open-air swimming pool.

Public bathhouses, such as the Baths of Caracalla *(inset)*, had large staffs. Some employees tended the furnaces and the water supply, keeping the pools and rooms at the proper temperatures. Others gave massages or handed out exercise equipment. Still others monitored the dressing rooms or gave out towels to the bathers.

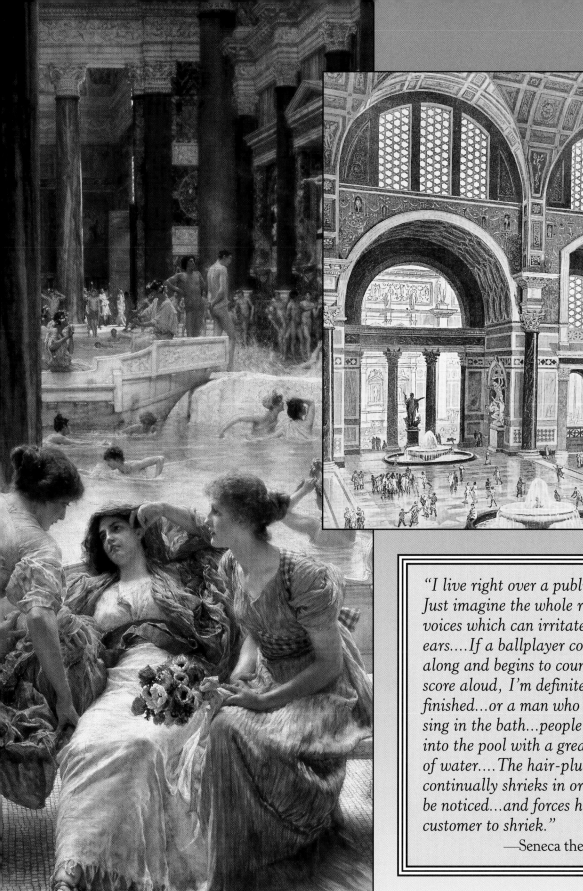

"I live right over a public bath. Just imagine the whole range of voices which can irritate my ears....If a ballplayer comes along and begins to count his score aloud, I'm definitely finished...or a man who loves to sing in the bath...people diving into the pool with a great splash of water....The hair-plucker continually shrieks in order to be noticed...and forces his customer to shriek."

—Seneca the Younger

"They who were once the gods of the nation dwell now with the owls and the bats under their lonely roofs."
—Saint Jerome

Rome Becomes Christian

The persecutions by Nero and later emperors did not stop the growth of Christianity. By the fourth century A.D., Christians made up 10 percent of Rome's population.

Christians came from all ranks of Roman society. They might be slaves, freed people, ordinary citizens, or even the wealthy. They were not, however, Romans of political power, for power was linked to the worship of the traditional state gods.

After death most non-Christian Romans were cremated, their bodies reduced to ashes by burning. But Christian beliefs required the dead to be buried, so their bodies would be preserved. Burials were not allowed within the city, so Christian cemeteries grew up outside the walls, sometimes on the property of a wealthy Christian. To preserve space, underground chambers, or catacombs, were cut into the soft rock that lay under Rome.

Many Christians came to pray at the tombs of martyrs. These people had died rather than renounce the Christian faith. Most revered was the tomb of the apostle Peter on Vatican Hill. Tradition held that, under Nero's orders, on this spot Peter had been persecuted and died.

Christians suffered some of the worst persecutions under the emperor Galerius. But on his deathbed in 311, this ruler regretted his actions and decreed that Christianity should be tolerated. More freedom for Christians came in 313, when the new emperor Constantine adopted Christianity as his own personal religion. He donated land and ordered the construction of a basilica, or public building, for Christian worship. Called the Basilica of St. John Lateran, this was the first church in Rome. In 326, Constantine had a basilica built on the site of Saint Peter's tomb on Vatican Hill.

The leader of the Christians and of the Roman Catholic Church came to be called the pope. Popes considered their authority to have been handed down from Saint Peter. Later in the fourth century, when Christianity became the state religion, the pope became a powerful state leader. Many Romans continued to worship traditional Roman gods until they were outlawed in 391.

Despite the spectacle of Christians slaughtered in the Colosseum *(left)*, the religion grew. Christians kneel in prayer at a catacomb funeral *(inset)*.

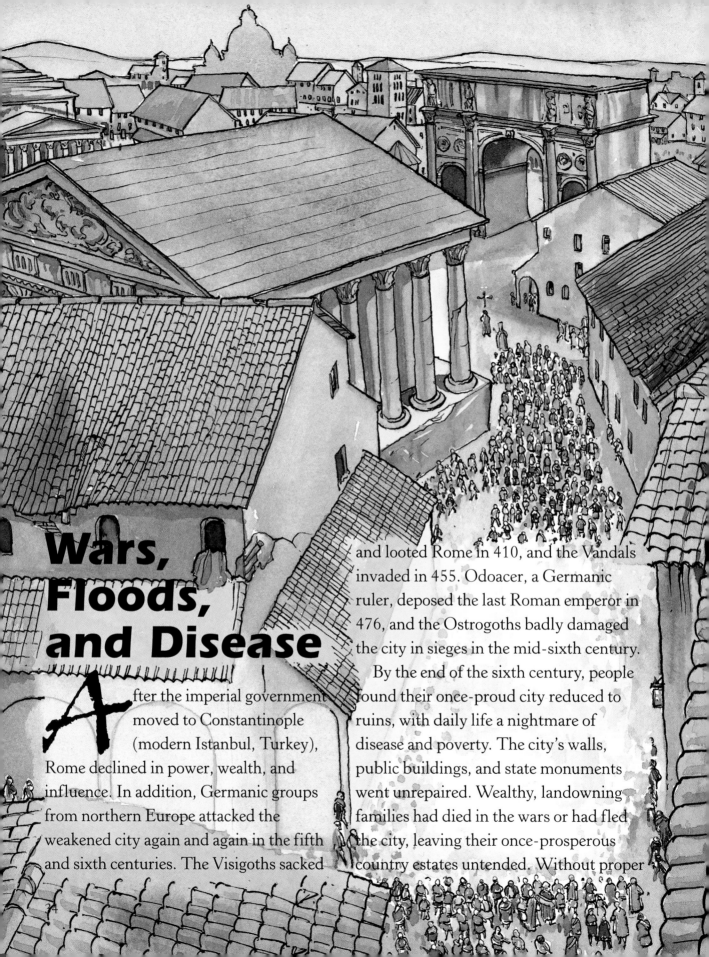

Wars, Floods, and Disease

After the imperial government moved to Constantinople (modern Istanbul, Turkey), Rome declined in power, wealth, and influence. In addition, Germanic groups from northern Europe attacked the weakened city again and again in the fifth and sixth centuries. The Visigoths sacked and looted Rome in 410, and the Vandals invaded in 455. Odoacer, a Germanic ruler, deposed the last Roman emperor in 476, and the Ostrogoths badly damaged the city in sieges in the mid-sixth century.

By the end of the sixth century, people found their once-proud city reduced to ruins, with daily life a nightmare of disease and poverty. The city's walls, public buildings, and state monuments went unrepaired. Wealthy, landowning families had died in the wars or had fled the city, leaving their once-prosperous country estates untended. Without proper

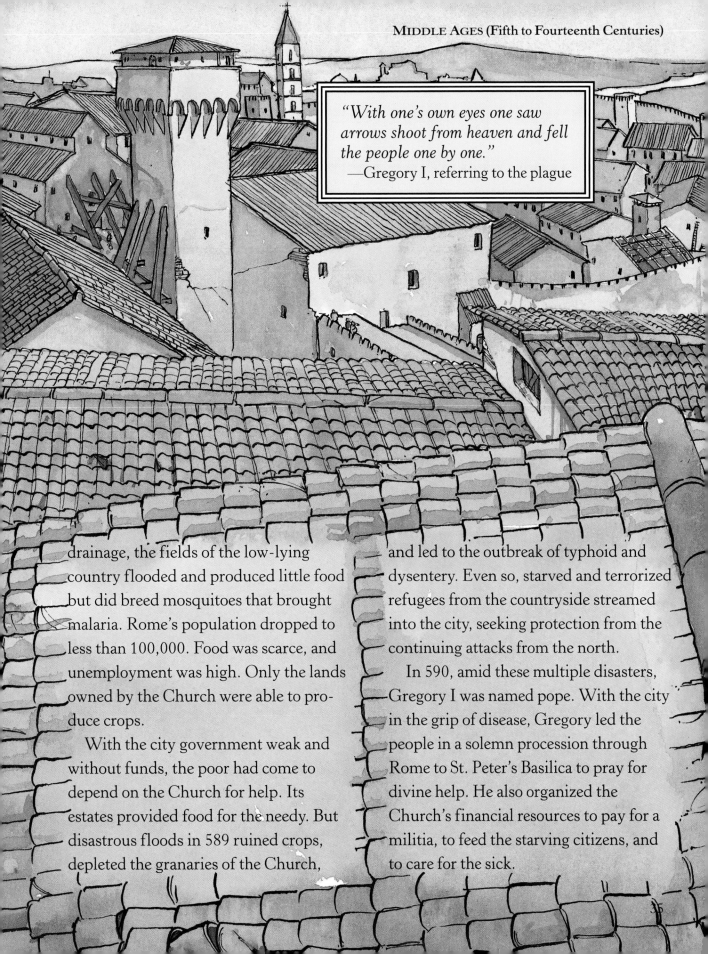

> *"With one's own eyes one saw arrows shoot from heaven and fell the people one by one."*
> —Gregory I, referring to the plague

drainage, the fields of the low-lying country flooded and produced little food but did breed mosquitoes that brought malaria. Rome's population dropped to less than 100,000. Food was scarce, and unemployment was high. Only the lands owned by the Church were able to produce crops.

With the city government weak and without funds, the poor had come to depend on the Church for help. Its estates provided food for the needy. But disastrous floods in 589 ruined crops, depleted the granaries of the Church,

and led to the outbreak of typhoid and dysentery. Even so, starved and terrorized refugees from the countryside streamed into the city, seeking protection from the continuing attacks from the north.

In 590, amid these multiple disasters, Gregory I was named pope. With the city in the grip of disease, Gregory led the people in a solemn procession through Rome to St. Peter's Basilica to pray for divine help. He also organized the Church's financial resources to pay for a militia, to feed the starving citizens, and to care for the sick.

Pilgrims Come to Rome

Since the early days of Christianity, pilgrims had come to Rome to visit the tombs of the martyrs. At first the travelers came from lands to the east, where Christianity had begun. But Pope Gregory I sent missionaries to convert the people of Britain and western Europe to the Roman Catholic faith, and by 600, thousands of pilgrims from lands west of Rome were arriving in the city.

Pilgrims came from all walks of life. Some were clergy, such as bishops, priests, monks, and nuns. Some were nobles. Some were chieftains and their followers. Many were ordinary people. They came to fulfill vows or to seek forgiveness for sins. Some, who were sick, made the pilgrimage in the hope of a cure. And all needed shelter and food.

Welfare centers and hospices—accommodations that the Church provided—could not handle the droves of pilgrims. Their arrival created jobs for many Romans. Innkeepers hired helpers to do the laundry and cleaning. Foodsellers and tavern keepers employed cooks and serving people and purchased supplies from local farmers. All manner of artisans and shopkeepers—clothing makers, cobblers, blacksmiths, and saddlers—found work.

Some Romans were guides or sold souvenirs of the pilgrimage. And although it was discouraged, the trade in sacred relics was popular. High prices could be asked for bits of bone, cloth, wood, or metal that were believed to be associated with a saint.

In 800 Pope Leo III sought help in defending Rome and the papacy. He chose the Frankish king Charlemagne, whose lands covered modern France and Germany. Charlemagne traveled to St. Peter's to be crowned Holy Roman Emperor on Christmas Day. But this occasion was not the first time Charlemagne had been in the basilica. A devout Christian, the king had already visited Rome as a pilgrim.

The pilgrims who came to Rome found themselves in the capital of western Christianity. At its center was the pope, who was both head of the Roman Catholic Church and the most powerful leader in Rome.

Field of Towers

A traveler who visited Rome during the Middle Ages thought the city looked like a "field of towers." He saw hundreds of defensive towers—some more than 100 feet tall—built to fortify the dwellings of the wealthy. From these strongholds, powerful families controlled the area and often fought among themselves.

Medieval Rome had two sections. Most of the city's 40,000 to 80,000 inhabitants lived in the Abitato, the densely populated area located along both sides of the bend in the Tiber River. A small, crowded area of narrow streets, the Abitato included the heart of the ancient city. Here wealthy and working-class Romans lived side by side. Often the poor built flimsy structures that leaned against the walls of sturdier buildings.

Wealthy families converted ancient monuments, such as the Colosseum and the Theater of Marcellus, into household compounds strengthened by the defensive towers. The family lived on upper floors and rented the ground level spaces to artisans or shopkeepers, who lived and worked on the premises. Butchers occupied many of the ground floor stalls at the Theater of Marcellus. The old Senate House had become a church. A congregation of monks owned the Circus Maximus and rented out the spaces below the seats as living quarters. The Forum, overgrown with vegetation, was called the "cow pasture."

Working-class Romans who could afford residences in the better part of town bought tiny row houses, consisting of one or two rooms and a small garden that perhaps held a fruit tree. Fruit trees are often mentioned in the record of the sale of property, so they may have been an important source of food or income.

The larger part of the city, called the Disabitato, consisted mostly of ruined fields, vineyards, pastures, and farms. Here and there, monks had converted a wealthy estate into a monastery. Occasional mansions, defended by towers, stood on the deserted hills and valleys.

With structures neglected and filled in by garbage and rubble, the glory of Rome had been all but forgotten by the city's dwindling medieval population.

First Holy Year

Pope Boniface VIII declared the year 1300 the first Holy Year. He decreed that pilgrims who visited Rome's shrines for 15 days would receive pardon for their sins. Romans, who did not have the burden of long travel, had to visit for 30 days. Most pilgrims donated something at each shrine.

Most of Rome's shrines lay outside the walls at the burial sites of martyrs. The pilgrims moved around the city, visiting the widely scattered churches devoted to Saints Peter, Paul, and John Lateran. Along the way were many smaller shrines, churches, and catacombs.

Although Rome was used to pilgrims, it had never hosted as many as the million or more who came during the Holy Year.

Traffic controls had to be set up to create order in the crowds crossing the bridge to St. Peter's Basilica. Inns ran out of rooms, and prices for lodging skyrocketed. Welfare centers were filled. Straw sellers in the courtyard of St. Peter's sold bedding to pilgrims who slept wherever they could. Rome's merchants profited from the crowds, and street vendors peddled candles, rosaries, and souvenirs.

Even the poorest pilgrims made donations at the shrines of beloved saints, and many left gifts of special value for this unique occasion. Some pilgrims were cheated out of their valuables by nobles who stopped visitors at the crossroads or bridges controlled by their towers. Still the first Holy Year was a success for the Roman Catholic Church, for Rome, and for the faithful who made the pilgrimage.

> "Leaving Rome on Christmas Eve I saw a great crowd....Several times I saw men and women trampled under the feet of others, and even I was in the same danger, only just escaping on several occasions. The pope received an untold amount of money from them, as day and night two priests stood at the altar of St. Paul's holding rakes in their hands, raking in infinite money....and I, William, was there, and earned fifty years and more of indulgence."
>
> —William Ventura

Cola di Rienzo, Hero of the People

Despite—or because of—Rome's growing prosperity, feuds among Rome's many powerful families or struggles between them and the pope often erupted. In the middle of the fourteenth century, the popes moved their residence to France for greater safety. No central authority was left in Rome to curb the abuses of the nobles. In 1313, into these disordered times, Cola di Rienzo was born.

The son of a tavern keeper, Rienzo was educated at the University of Rome, where he was inspired by stories of the ancient city. He dreamed of restoring the rule of ordinary citizens and of renewing the glory of Rome. On an errand to the pope in France, he persuaded the Roman Catholic leader to support his cause.

Upon his return to Rome, Rienzo organized a citizens' revolt, and the nobles fled. But Rienzo's grandiose ideas and high taxes soon dimmed the people's enthusiasm for their new civic leader. Even though Rienzo's forces defeated a gathering of nobles at the gate of San Lorenzo in 1347, the pope withdrew his support. In spite of Rienzo's victory, the people would not back a leader of whom the pope did not approve. Nor did they want to disrupt plans for the second Holy Year, declared for 1350. Rienzo left the city. When the Holy Year ended, the nobles were more lawless than ever. In the summer of 1354, a new pope invited Rienzo to help regain Rome. Rienzo returned, and the people welcomed him as a hero.

But again his popularity was short lived. The citizens rebelled against Rienzo's overblown idea of himself and especially against his high taxes. In October 1354, mobs attacked Rienzo's residence, shouting "Death to the traitor!" With his house afire, Rienzo covered his fine clothing with an ordinary cloak and attempted to flee. But the jewelry he had forgotten to take off betrayed his identity. He was discovered and murdered. For two days, his body hung outside the house of one of his bitterest enemies. Cola di Rienzo's dream had failed. And disorder ruled the city until 1377, when the pope returned to Rome.

43

Carnival

Carnival, held just before Lent (a period of fasting before Easter), was a time for fun and games that lasted for days. Throughout the city, costumed Romans danced and feasted. The revelers attended games, parties, and spectacles.

Carnival games had been held on Testaccio Hill, at the southern end of town, since the Middle Ages. During the celebrations, races of all kinds, including footraces, were among the most popular games. In one notable event, pigs were packed into carts and rolled off the hill to crash at the bottom, where people waited to grab them.

Pope Paul II added an exciting new event to Carnival in 1466, when he sponsored a race of Arabian horses through one of the main streets of the city. Once untied, the riderless horses galloped along the thoroughfare, which came to be called Via del Corso (Race Street). A large sheet draped across the street stopped the horses at the end of the mile-long race.

Pageants and parades of elaborate floats were also part of Carnival. As Romans started to take an interest in their city's ancient past, festivals began to include classical themes, with replicas of Roman chariots and even Roman gods and goddesses. In 1513 one spectacular float featured a sphere, representing the world. When it split apart, a young woman representing Rome emerged, releasing a flock of birds.

In 1545 the pope urged that the rowdy games on Testaccio Hill be replaced with more refined Carnival events. In a pageant of the same year, one float depicted the classical story of the hero Androcles removing a thorn from a lion's paw. Spectators understood that Androcles symbolized the pope and that the thorn being removed stood for heresy, or religious teachings of which the church did not approve.

An ancient version of Mardi Gras, Carnival was a time for Romans to party before Lent.

"Only a minority of the Roman people are Romans."
—Marcello Alberini, Roman official

Sleeping area

Living quarters

A goldsmith's workshop and salesroom

46

Rome and Its People in 1527

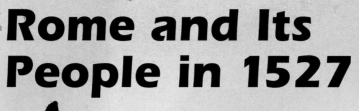

According to a census taken in 1526 and 1527, approximately 55,000 people lived in Rome. Only about one-fourth of them had been born in the city. The rest were from other parts of Italy or from European countries, mostly Spain, France, and the German states.

The census counted 21 households that contained 50 or more persons. The biggest establishment—belonging to the pope—numbered in the hundreds. Other large households were the property of wealthy cardinals and of nobles. The noble estates were self-contained farms, where servants, agricultural workers, and craftspeople lived and worked.

But most households were much smaller, with perhaps five to seven individuals—a husband and wife, their children, and other relatives. Many of these families were the shopkeepers and craftspeople of Rome. With living quarters above or behind the work area, wives and daughters often helped with the work, and sons learned the trade of the father.

Many workers were organized into trade or craft guilds (associations). Besides regulating the practice of the craft, many guilds helped members in other ways. Some made loans, or provided poor women with dowries (the money or goods a woman brought to her marriage), or helped families with medical or burial expenses.

Guilds also served as friendly social organizations, and some wealthy guilds even built churches for their members. However, only a few guilds were large and wealthy. Among them were the landowning stock breeders' guild, the jewelers with their luxury trade, and the bakers, whose work of milling flour and baking bread fed the city.

But most guilds were of only modest means. They represented small-scale trades, such as shoemaking, poultry selling, or secondhand merchandising. Because these guilds were subject to the control of both church and city officials, they had little political influence in sixteenth-century Rome. Most of the city's wealth and power lay with high church officials and important bankers, who did not belong to guilds.

Rebuilding St. Peter's

By the 1500s, when Rome began its Renaissance (rebirth), some of its buildings were growing very old. St. Peter's Basilica was almost 1,200 years old and in danger of collapse. The pope ordered repairs. But the idea of repairs soon gave way to the plan for a completely new church.

Many fine architects and artists of Renaissance Italy were already at work throughout the city, building and decorating churches, palaces, and monuments for wealthy patrons. The architect Donato Bramante employed 2,500 artisans and laborers. Before he died in 1514, Bramante had set into place four supports for a huge dome.

The gifted young painter Raphael was then put in charge of construction. But the work moved slowly, for Raphael was already occupied with the creation of many beautiful wall frescoes for the pope's palace in the Vatican. And by 1520, the artist had died.

In May 1527, the undisciplined troops of the Holy Roman Emperor Charles V sacked Rome. Thousands of men, women, and children, even nuns in their convents, were killed. Other citizens fled to the countryside. Those who could took refuge, along with the pope and high church officials, in the fortress of Sant' Angelo near St. Peter's. For days the troops murdered and looted. When they left, the city had been reduced to half its former population, and four-fifths of its houses had been destroyed.

In 1546, when work on St. Peter's resumed, the pope gave the task to the brilliant artist Michelangelo, then 72 years old. As a young man, Michelangelo had painted the scenes on the ceiling of the Vatican's Sistine Chapel. He set about designing the new basilica and enlarging its dome. When he died in 1564, the dome's walls had been raised, but the dome was still unroofed. Not until 1590 did workers complete the great dome of St. Peter's, the largest in the world.

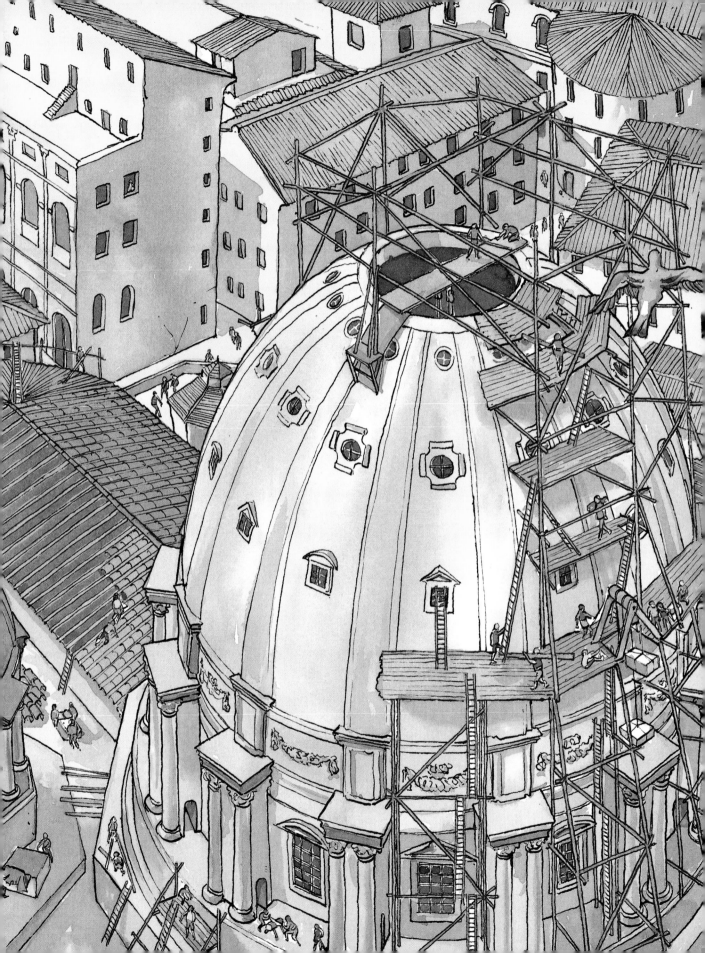

Renaissance Women

The women of Renaissance Rome lived in a male-dominated society where fathers and husbands made all important decisions. Most women married at a young age, often to husbands chosen by their parents. Wives were expected to bear children, manage the household, and help their husbands however they could. Girls in wealthier families were tutored in music and trained in needlework.

But not all women married. A woman who had no dowry was unlikely to find a marriage partner. Sometimes guilds or other charitable organizations gave dowries to poor young women so they could marry. Unmarried or widowed women often entered the convent, where girls as young as six or seven were also placed if there was no money for dowries or if the family had many daughters. Many of the women in convents were

there not because they wanted to be nuns but because they had nowhere else to go. Convents often served as orphanages or refuges for unattached women.

But many women chose to be nuns for spiritual and religious reasons. They wanted to lead a life of prayer or to care for the poor and the sick. Or a woman might choose a convent where learning was stressed. Some nuns were highly educated and taught others. Most girls who were educated during the Renaissance received their schooling in convents.

Roman society at this time offered women no respectable roles outside of the Church or the family. A woman on her own—especially if she was pursuing a career—was viewed with suspicion and often treated with disrespect.

Confined to the convent or secluded within the family structure, women lived, almost without exception, under the authority of others. Aside from persuasion, there was little they could do to influence the decisions that affected their lives.

The Grand Tour

In the eighteenth century, as part of their education, wealthy young men from Britain visited Rome on a "Grand Tour" of European cities. As schoolboys they had read the classical Roman authors and had learned the history of the ancient city. Some of these visitors found their imaginations deeply stirred. James Boswell, a young Scot who visited in 1765, felt "melancholy emotions" overcome him when he viewed the Forum "all in ruins, with the wretched huts of carpenters and other artisans occupying the site." But Rome was not all ruins and classical history for Boswell. He also visited the Vatican Library, marveled at Michelangelo's statue of Moses, went to the church where Cola di Rienzo had been crowned, and watched as the pope washed the feet of 12 priests in a Lenten ceremony. He wrote, too, of young girls going off to become nuns.

Some visitors complained of the noisy, crowded streets. But to most, the sights, sounds, smells, and tastes of Rome were fascinating. Travelers wrote of the friendly, hospitable Romans, the wonderful food, and the inexpensive accommodations. They participated in Carnival celebrations, went to the theater, browsed at the booksellers, and met friends in the wineshops.

But amid all the city's pleasures, some British visitors could not forget Rome's past. Edward Gibbon wrote that he could "never forget nor express the strong emotions which agitated" him so much he could not sleep. As he sat among some neglected Roman ruins one October evening in 1764, the idea came to him of writing the history of Rome. The result was his famous work, *The History of the Decline and Fall of the Roman Empire,* which has long molded the image of ancient Rome.

Many writers and artists from Europe found Rome an exciting place to live and work. They visited the awe-inspiring Pantheon *(inset)* and sketched and pondered the ruins in the Campo Vaccino *(left)*. "Only now do I begin to live," the German poet Johann von Goethe exclaimed when he arrived in 1786.

The Capital of Italy

After a brief occupation by the French in the early 1800s, Rome had returned to papal rule. But in February 1849, an assembly of the people declared a new Roman Republic, which would be independent of the pope's authority. The new leader, Giuseppe Mazzini, hoped that the revolt of Rome would spark the liberation of Italy and the creation of a single Italian state with Rome as its capital.

Giuseppe Garibaldi *(inset)*, a dashing and heroic guerrilla fighter, shared Mazzini's dreams. In 1849 Garibaldi and his men, called the "Red Shirts," entered Rome just as the French were sending troops to aid the pope. Garibaldi attracted many new followers, including students, professors, artists, workers, and sailors. Some were Romans. Others were from foreign lands. Led by Garibaldi, the volunteer soldiers successfully defended their position at the city walls on April 30, 1849. But in a later battle, the untrained militia proved no match for the disciplined French troops.

In early July, Garibaldi left Rome, taking 4,000 volunteers with him to continue the fight for liberation throughout Italy. At last the country was united under King Victor Emmanuel II of Sardinia, an island off the coast of the peninsula. In 1861 Rome was named the capital of Italy, and in 1871 the king moved his court to the city. The pope, no longer ruler of Rome or of the Papal States (the church's lands in central Italy), withdrew to the precincts of the Vatican. The discord between the pope and the king divided the loyalties of many Romans.

In spite of political conflicts, Roman workers continued to improve and modernize the city. Crews built embankments along the Tiber to prevent flooding and to widen streets. Trains linked Rome with the outside world. Laborers completed a steel drawbridge across the river. The new construction exposed many ancient ruins, and the government called on archaeologists to help excavate and preserve important monuments.

Within view of St. Peter's Basilica, fishing crews work the banks of the Tiber.

54

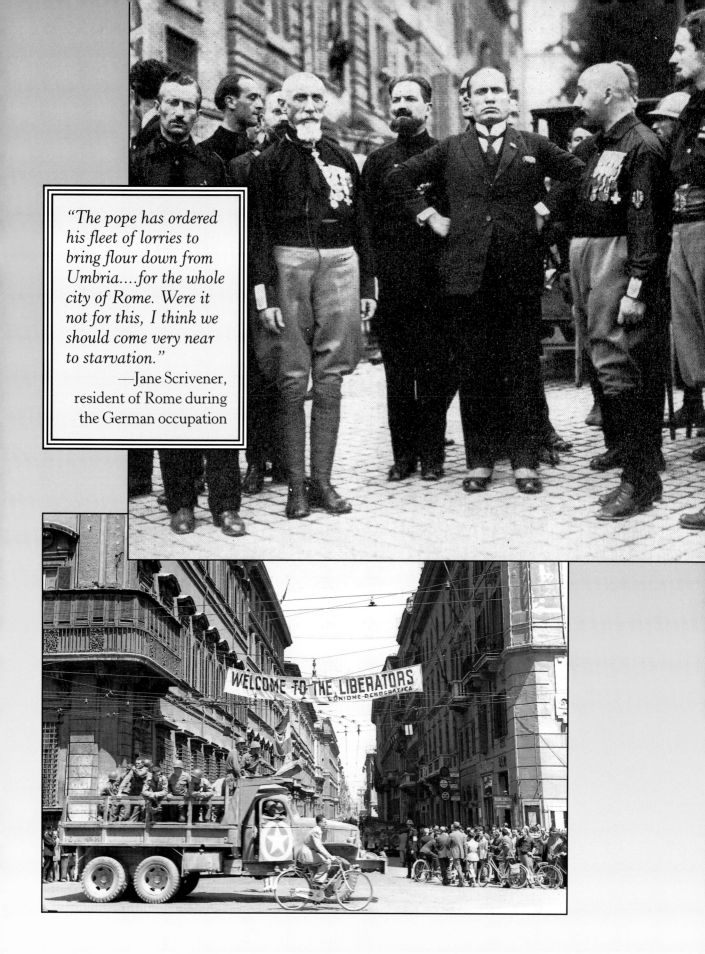

"The pope has ordered his fleet of lorries to bring flour down from Umbria....for the whole city of Rome. Were it not for this, I think we should come very near to starvation."

—Jane Scrivener, resident of Rome during the German occupation

The Early Twentieth Century

As the capital of Italy, Rome quickly grew to almost half a million people. Many of the residents were poor people from the countryside. They had come looking for work in the many construction projects that multiplied in the 1920s and 1930s.

At that time, Benito Mussolini, leader of the Fascist Party, was prime minister of Italy. He wanted to make Rome a grand capital, as it had been under Augustus, and set to work to transform the city. Crews created new streets and widened old ones. The government employed many citizens in these public works.

In 1929 the long-standing problem of defining the authority of the Church in Rome was finally resolved under the terms of the Lateran Treaty. This agreement was between the Italian government and the Roman Catholic Church. The pact established the Vatican, along with several other Church territories in Rome, as an independent country called Vatican City, with the pope as its ruler.

During World War II (1939–1945), Mussolini placed Italy on the side of Germany. Under Nazi Party leader Adolf Hitler, Germany had plunged much of Europe into war. Never popular, Mussolini was finally removed from power in 1943. When Italy surrendered to the Allies (the anti-German alliance), Nazi forces occupied Rome.

Between 1943 and 1944, Romans endured repression, hunger, cold, and bombings while they waited for the Allies to free the city. Half a million refugees from the war-torn countryside sought shelter in the capital. Citizens took them in and shared their meager provisions. Bread, which was severely rationed, was often the only food available.

Air raids killed and injured thousands of Romans and destroyed almost 2,500 homes. Italian resistance efforts only brought more Nazi repression. On June 5, 1944, the Allied troops entered Rome, and jubilant Romans showered their liberators with roses.

(Top) Benito Mussolini *(hands on hips)* and members of his fledgling Fascist Party pose soon after they marched on Rome. *(Left)* World War II ended for Rome when U.S. troops entered the city in June of 1944.

Modern Rome

Modern Rome is the capital of the Republic of Italy, which includes the islands of Sicily and Sardinia in the Mediterranean Sea. Established after World War II, the city's government is democratic. Representatives are elected, and women have the right to vote.

Rome is home to many international corporations and businesses. Since 1950 it has housed the headquarters of the UN's Food and Agriculture Organization. Important libraries and international educational centers are located in the city. And Vatican City is enclosed within Rome's city limits.

In 1960 Rome hosted the Summer Olympic Games. To facilitate the international event, the government built a new Olympic stadium to seat 100,000 spectators and an Olympic Village to house 6,000 athletes from 84 countries.

Some sports were held at ancient sites throughout the city. Wrestlers contended in the ruins of a basilica, and gymnasts competed in the remains of a public bath. The closing marathon took runners along the ancient cobblestones of the Appian Way, built in the days of the first Roman Republic. Passing through the Forum, the racers ended at the Arch of Constantine, in sight of the Colosseum.

As it has for centuries, Rome welcomes visitors, and tourism is one of the city's main industries. Estimates suggest that 20 to 40 million people may visit Rome in 2000, which Pope John Paul II has declared a Holy Year. The city plans to complete a new subway line to St. Peter's in time for the event.

These days more than three million people live in metropolitan Rome. Many reside in suburbs that have developed around the old "city of the seven hills." Some live in the Olympic Village, which was converted to housing after the games ended. In the city center, ancient monuments have been cleared of debris and restored. Archaeological excavations are ongoing, bringing to light new information about the city's history.

Rome remains a city of bold and spirited architecture, both ancient and modern. This eighteenth-century house captures the festive and daring spirit of Rome.

Rome Timeline

	First Millennium B.C.	First Millennium A.D.
1000 B.C.–753 B.C. Iron Age	**753 B.C.** Rome founded (traditional date)	
753 B.C.–509 B.C. Etruscan Domination	**6TH/7TH C.B.C.** Etruscan kings **509 B.C.** Roman Republic established	
509 B.C.–27 B.C. Roman Republic	**390 B.C.** Gauls sack Rome **264 B.C.** First Punic War begins **241 B.C.** First Punic War ends—Rome acquires Sicily **238 B.C.** Rome acquires Sardinia and Corsica **218 B.C.** Second Punic War begins **216 B.C.** Rome defeated by Hannibal at Cannae **204 B.C.** Rome imports goddess Cybele **201 B.C.** Second Punic War ends **146 B.C.** Rome destroys Carthage **135–132 B.C.** Slaves revolt in Sicily **104–101 B.C.** Slaves revolt again in Sicily **89 B.C.** Roman citizenship extended to all Italians **73–71 B.C.** Spartacus leads slave revolt in Italy **51 B.C.** Rome controls Gaul **44 B.C.** Julius Caesar assassinated **31 B.C.** Octavian (later Augustus) defeats Antony and Cleopatra at Actium; Rome gains Egypt	
27 B.C.–A.D. 476 Roman Empire	**27 B.C.** Octavian named emperor, called Augustus	**A.D. 43** Rome controls Britain **A.D. 64** Great Fire of Rome; Nero persecutes Christians **A.D. 80** Colosseum opens **A.D. 197** Soldiers receive right to marry **A.D. 212** Roman citizenship extended to all freemen and freewomen throughout empire **A.D. 217** Baths of Caracalla built **A.D. 275** Aurelian Wall built around Rome **A.D. 311** Emperor Galerius issues edict of toleration for Christians **A.D. 313** Constantine accepts Christianity **A.D. 315** Arch of Constantine built **A.D. 326** St. Peter's Basilica built **A.D. 330** Capital of empire moved to Constantinople **A.D. 391** Worship of Roman gods outlawed **A.D. 395** Empire divided into east and west **A.D. 410** Visigoths sack Rome **A.D. 455** Vandals sack Rome **A.D. 476** Last western emperor deposed

A.D. 476–A.D. 1300 Medieval Rome	A.D. 590	Gregory I becomes pope	
	A.D. 595	Gregory sends missionaries to Britain and Europe	
	A.D. 800	Charlemagne crowned Holy Roman Emperor of Rome	
	A.D. 854	Defensive wall built around St. Peter's	
			A.D. 1143 — Romans revolt against nobles, establish Commune of Rome
			A.D. 1300 — First Holy Year
A.D. 1300–A.D. 1600 Renaissance Rome			A.D. 1308 — Pope leaves Rome, moves to France
			A.D. 1350 — Second Holy Year
			A.D. 1354 — Cola di Rienzo murdered
			A.D. 1377 — Pope returns to live at Rome
			A.D. 1450 (ca.) — Vatican Library founded
			A.D. 1466 — First horse races in Via del Corso
			A.D. 1506 — Rebuilding St. Peter's begins
			A.D. 1512 — Michelangelo finishes ceiling of Sistine Chapel
			A.D. 1527 — Sack of Rome by troops of Charles V
			A.D. 1564 — Michelangelo dies; walls of St. Peter's dome completed
			A.D. 1590 — Dome of St. Peter's completed
A.D. 1600– Modern Rome			A.D. 1764 — Edward Gibbon visits Rome
			A.D. 1765 — James Boswell visits Rome
			A.D. 1808 — French occupy Rome
			A.D. 1810 — French begin archaeological excavation in the Forum
			A.D. 1849 — Guiseppe Garibaldi and liberation fighters leave Rome
			A.D. 1860 — First railroad in Rome
			A.D. 1861 — Rome named capital of united Italy
			A.D. 1922 — Mussolini becomes prime minister
			A.D. 1944 — Rome liberated by Allies
			A.D. 1946 — Republic of Italy established
			A.D. 1960 — Rome hosts Summer Olympics
			A.D. 2000 — Holy Year

Books about Italy and Rome

Bisignano, Alphonse. *Cooking the Italian Way.* Minneapolis: Lerner Publications Company, 1982.

Chrisp, Peter. *The Romans.* New York: Chelsea House Publishers, 1994.

Clare, John D., ed. *Classical Rome.* San Diego, CA: Harcourt Brace Jovanovich, 1993.

Corbishley, Mike. *Everyday Life in Roman Times.* New York: Franklin Watts, 1994.

Corbishley, Mike. *What Do We Know About the Romans?* New York: Peter Bedrick Books, 1991.

Dazzling! Jewelry of the Ancient World. Minneapolis: Runestone Press, 1994.

Dineen, Jacqueline. *The Romans.* Old Tappan, NJ: Simon & Schuster Children's, 1992.

Fired Up! Making Pottery in Ancient Times. Minneapolis: Runestone Press, 1993.

Howarth, Sarah. *Roman People.* Brookfield, CT: The Millbrook Press, 1995.

Italy in Pictures. Minneapolis: Lerner Publications Company, 1997.

James, Simon. *Ancient Rome.* An Eyewitness Book. New York: Alfred A. Knopf, Inc. 1990.

James, Simon. *Ancient Rome.* New York: Viking Penguin, 1992.

Nardo, Don. *The Roman Republic.* San Diego, CA: Lucent Books, Inc. 1997.

Piece by Piece! Mosaics of the Ancient World. Minneapolis: Runestone Press, 1993.

Schneider, Mical. *Between the Dragon and the Eagle.* Minneapolis: Carolrhoda Books, Inc., 1996.

Sold! The Origins of Money and Trade. Minneapolis: Runestone Press, 1994.

Street Smart! Cities of the Ancient World. Minneapolis: Runestone Press, 1994.

Index

About the Author and Illustrator

Joan Barghusen worked for many years as director of museum education for the Oriental Institute of the University of Chicago. Her interest in ancient Mediterranean civilizations has taken her to Tunisia and Malta, where she helped with museum education projects. She has written widely, most lately for *Cricket* magazine. She is working on a book about ancient Carthage.

Ray Webb of Woodstock, England, studied art and design at Birmingham Polytechnic in Birmingham, England. A specialist in historical and scientific subjects, his work has been published in Great Britain, the Netherlands, Germany, and the United States. He still finds time to teach young people interested in becoming illustrators.

Acknowledgments

For quoted material: p. 9, Jo-Ann Shelton. *As the Romans Did.* (New York: Oxford University Press, 1988); p. 15 (top), Mike Corbishley. *What Do We Know about the Romans?* (New York: Peter Bedrick Books, 1991); pp. 15 (bottom), 17, 18, 23, Shelton, *As the Romans Did;* p. 24, Christopher Hibbert. *Rome.* (New York: W. W. Norton, 1985); p. 27, B. W. Henderson. *The Life and Principate of the Emperor Nero.* (Rome: Lerma di Bretschneider, 1968); pp. 28, 31, Shelton, *As the Romans Did;* p. 32, Hibbert, Rome; p. 35, Peter Llewellyn. *Rome in the Dark Ages.* (New York: Praeger Publishers, 1970); p. 41, Paul Hetherington. *Medieval Rome.* (New York: St. Martin's Press, 1994); p. 46, Peter Partner. *Renaissance Rome.* (Berkeley, CA: University of California Press, 1980); p. 53, Hibbert, *Rome;* p. 56, Jane Scrivener. *Inside Rome with the Germans.* (New York: Macmillan, 1945).

For photos: Scala/Art Resource, NY, p. 7; Bridgeman Art Library, pp. 9, 11, 20–21, 28, 30–31, 36, 45, 52, 55; Bettmann, p. 11 (inset); Corbis-Bettmann, pp. 12, 26–27, 31 (inset), 32 (inset); Stock Montage, Inc., pp. 12 (inset), 20, 28 (inset), 55 (inset), 56 (top); UPI/Corbis-Bettmann, pp. 32, 56 (bottom); © Erich Lessing/Art Resource, NY, p. 39; Ancient Art & Architecture Collection, Ltd., p. 52 (inset); PhotoDisc, pp. 58, 59. Cover photo: © Erich Lessing/Art Resource, NY.